Photo Credits:
Color: Dr. G. Allen: 14 (below); Dr. Herbert R. Axelrod: 6, 7, 15, 66, 71, 83, 86, 87; John Chelman & Dorothy Petrulla: 10, 11, 18, 22, 23, 26, 27, 30, 31 (top), 70, 74, 75, 90, 91, 94; Horst Mueller: 14 (top), 19, 78 (top); San Diego Zoo: 78 (below), 82; L. Robinson: 79; Dr. Matthew M. Vriends: 2, 3, 27 (below), 31 (below).

Black and White: Dr. Herbert R. Axelrod: 48; John Chelman & Dorothy Petrulla: 21, 24, 39, 50, 51, 55, 56, 57, 73, 77; Kerry V. Donnelly: 25, 40, 41; Harry V. Lacey: 5, 13, 16, 17, 20, 35, 60, 61, 72.

Front endpapers: A scarlet-chested parakeet *(Neophema splendida)*. This bird may be kept with Bourke's parakeets, cockatiels and many other species. During the breeding season, however, a pair is best kept on its own. Photo by Dr. Matthew M. Vriends.

Back endpapers: The turquoisine grass parakeet.

t.f.h.

0-87666-982-8

Distributed in the U.S. by T.F.H. Publications, Inc., 211 West Sylvania Avenue, P.O. Box 427, Neptune, N.J. 07753; in England by T.F.H. (Gt. Britain) Ltd., 13 Nutley Lane, Reigate, Surrey; in Canada to the book store and library trade by Beaverbooks, 953 Dillingham Road, Pickering, Ontario L1W 1Z7; in Canada to the pet trade by Rolf C. Hagen Ltd., 3225 Sartelon Street, Montreal 382, Quebec; in Southeast Asia by Y.W. Ong, 9 Lorong 36 Geylang, Singapore 14; in Australia and the South Pacific by Pet Imports Pty. Ltd., P.O. Box 149, Brookvale 2100, N.S.W., Australia; in South Africa by Valiant Publishers (Pty.) Ltd., P.O. Box 78236, Sandton City, 2146, South Africa; Published by T.F.H. Publications, Inc., Ltd., The British Crown Colony of Hong Kong.

Breeding the Colorful Little
GRASS PARAKEET

by RALPH SMITH

A turquoisine grass parakeet *(Neophema pulchella)*. This beautiful bird becomes active toward the evening; it is a bird of the twilight. The cock (photo) sings a soft whistling song.

The behavior of the turquoisine is most charming in early spring when it begins nesting plans.

ACKNOWLEDGMENTS

I feel that it is only appropriate at this point to thank the many, many friends who have helped me along the way through all these many years of breeding birds, and I'd like to add a special note of thanks to my wife, Mary Louise. Although not a breeder herself, she has many times taken over the care of the birds in emergencies and done a fine job, and she has been of tremendous help in my endeavor to pass my bird knowledge on to others.

A special note of thanks is expressed for the efforts of Dr. Ralph Cooper, who has always been standing by when help was needed in diagnosing the ailments of individual birds and prescribing appropriate medications.

FOREWORD

Although there are many bird breeders in the United States and especially in my area, southern California, who are successfully breeding grass parakeets, there is no single book that I know of that passes on breeding information to novice breeders. Most books containing information about grass parakeets dwell primarily on the birds' habits in the wild. They list such things as where the birds come from and what they look like and give their scientific names and taxonomic placement, plus other pertinent information. This information is of course necessary to give a true picture of the birds.

Novice breeders of grass parakeets, however, need other important information if they are to be successful in breeding these delightful and colorful little Australian birds without experiencing all of the costly disappointments and breeding failures otherwise experienced while slowly learning by trial and error, as most of us have done in the past.

It is my desire to remind readers that this book merely passes along information that I have obtained during the last several years through both reading and my actual experiences in breeding these dainty little birds. I've had many sad and costly experiences along the way—but I've also had many delightful and stimulating experiences, too. My breeding results year after year have been improving, and I seem to be on the right track. In this book I've tried to put all the pertinent facts in their true perspective, and I hope that I've succeeded in making the book easy to use and helpful for novice breeders.

Pied mutation of Bourke's parakeet raised at Turquoisine Aviaries.

One of the yellow mutations of the Bourke's parakeet hatched and fledged at the Turquoisine Aviaries.

Pied mutation of Bourke's parakeet. This mutation is one of several efforts being carried on at Turquoisine Aviaries.

The elegant grass parakeet *(Neophema elegans)* is a delightful aviary inhabitant.

11

I am not a veterinarian, nor do I have any degrees in ornithology or medicine. Most of the knowledge I have has been acquired through several years of breeding grass parakeets and studying their individual habits. For this reason, it is probably best at this point to state that any medication data or other technical data furnished in this book have been passed on to me by people who were qualified to do so.

The methods recommended in this book have been learned by trial and error. Additionally, many friends and breeders along the way have contributed generously and often of their own helpful ideas.

As you probably know by now, if you ask ten breeders how they raise their birds, you will probably receive ten different methods used to achieve the same results. This is one of the important reasons that I am now stating that this book is not meant to be critical of—nor do I have any argument with—any other breeders, regardless of the method used by them.

This book is meant to be a source of information for new breeders. Hopefully it will allow them to use the information contained in successfully raising the delightful and beautiful grass parakeets as I am doing, without encountering the pitfalls that new breeders usually encounter. It is hoped that the new breeders will keep an open mind as they progress with their breeding endeavors, being aware that new methods, procedures, medications, breeding techniques, etc., are constantly being announced and that new and better results therefore can and will be obtained. Among the saddest things that have happened to me in the past have been my encounters with the (very few, luckily) experienced but obstinate breeders who are solidly set in their methods and keep their minds closed to techniques used by others. I strive each day to remind myself to constantly keep an open mind—and I hope you will too.

Red-rumped parakeets (*Psephotus h. haematonotus*) are ideal foster-parents for all the grass parakeets. These parakeets may be kept in a large aviary with other birds, but not with their own kind. Their origin is southern and southeastern Australia.

Above left: Male blue-winged grass parakeet (*Neophema chrysostomus*). **Above right:** Male elegant grass parakeet (*N. elegans*). **Below:** A female Bourke's parakeet feeding a youngster. **Opposite:** The turquoisine grass parakeet is from New South Wales, Victoria and South Australia.

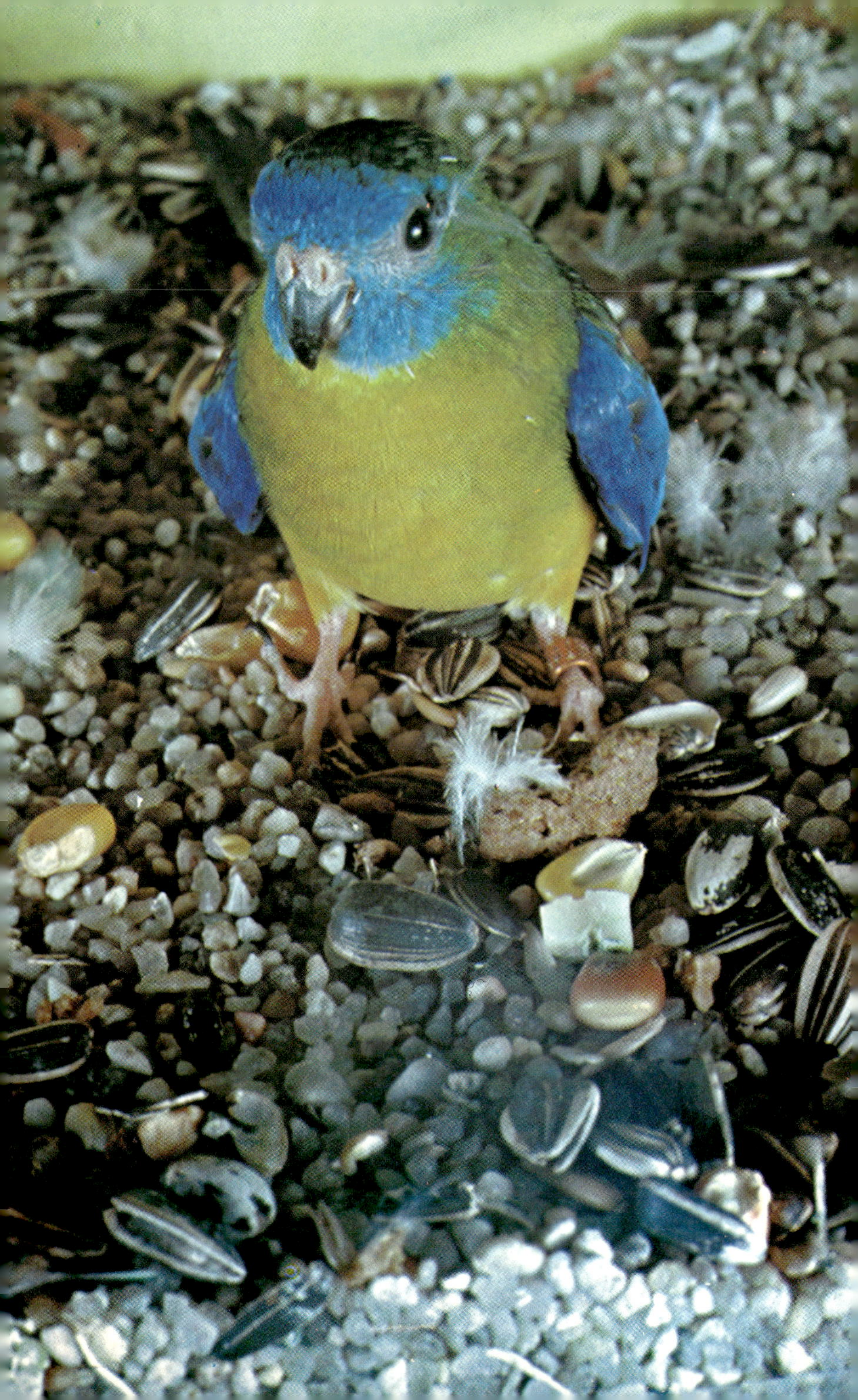

Bourke's parakeet has the habit of coming to drink at waterholes well before dawn and a few hours after sunset. Below: young elegant parakeets.

Grass Parakeets in General

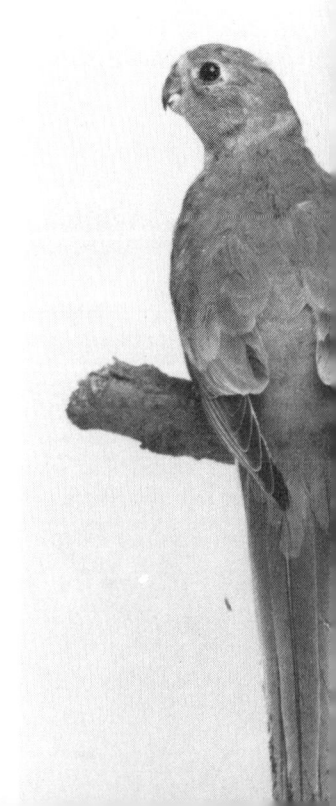

Grass parakeets all belong to the family Psittacidae, a large family of birds within the order Psittaciformes. There are seven grass parakeet species generally recognized: **the blue-winged grass parakeet** *(Neonanodes chrysostomus,* also known as *Neophema chrysostoma);* **the orange-bellied grass parakeet** *(Neophema chrysogaster);* **the rock grass parakeet** *(Neophema petrophila);* **the scarlet-chested, or splendid, grass parakeet** *(Neophema splendida);* **the turquoisine grass parakeet** *(Neophema pulchella);* **the elegant grass parakeet** *(Neophema elegans,* also known as *Neonanodes elegans);* and **Bourke's grass parakeet** *(Neophema bourkii,* also known as *Neopsephotus bourkii).*

A beautiful mutation of the scarlet-chested grass parakeet. This mutation is being developed at the Turquoisine Aviaries to produce an all red-fronted bird.

The scarlet-chested grass parakeet on the right is yellow-pied on the wings with white in the primaries. Even a completely yellow bird with a red breast was shown at one of the Dutch exhibitions in 1978.

Old turquoisine parakeets frequently show orange-red markings on the abdomen and are then often mistaken for scarlet-chested parakeets.

As you have probably already noticed, three of the seven species are referred to by more than one taxonomic name. The "correct" scientific names of birds depend on which book you pick up and read. Obviously, the taxonomists do not agree—just as many of us breeders do not agree on how these aviary gems should be raised. I shall therefore endeavor to stay clear of disagreement about nomenclature as I go along.

The last four species mentioned, starting with the scarlet-chested parakeet, are the ones to be referred to in this book, as they are the ones that are raised by many breeders in the United States, especially here in southern California. I must confess that I am not familiar with the first three species and therefore will not mention them again, as this book is meant to be a complete written essay of the methods used mostly by myself and a few others in successfully breeding these quiet, beautiful, and delightful aviary gems.

Pied mutation of Bourke's parakeet. The wild species is not at all uncommon in the wild, contrary to most reports.

An aviary under repair. This aviary (7' high, 7' wide and 40' long) was used by the author in colony-breeding Bourke's parakeet. Thirteen hens and ten cocks fledged thirty-seven chicks in 1978 at Turquoisine Aviaries.

Grass parakeet breeding facilities at Turquoisine Aviaries. All parrots are "carpenters" that will quickly reduce soft wood aviaries and perches to matchwood and will damage or destroy all shrubs and plants. Hence you must protect all woodwork with wire netting.

23

Height in an aviary is important, because most birds naturally like to fly up and also to roost as well as to nest in the upper portions of the enclosure.

Housing

Housing is one of the most controversial subjects that can be encountered in discussing bird breeding with other breeders. I therefore will try to describe how and why I built my aviaries and let the new breeder-to-be take it from there.

Most of my pens are two feet, eight inches wide. I would much prefer a minimum width of four feet, but being confined to a small area to build in, I had no other choice. For small birds such as grass parakeets, it has worked out very well. Some breeders are breeding them in pens two feet and even one foot, six inches wide. If the pens are too wide the breeder will have trouble in netting the birds. Trapping areas are built to solve this problem.

A double row of breeding pens at Turquoisine Aviaries. One pen is 7′ high, 2′ 8″ wide and 8′ long.

Bourke's and redrump parakeets. These are among the most popular of Australian parakeets. Both species are very attractive and easily bred.

Dr. Matthew Vriends' aviaries for small grass parakeets and larger species.

Now might be a good time to mention the fact that larger birds need larger pens than the smaller birds, especially in the width and length of the pen. If the new pens are built narrow and short and at a later date the new breeder decides to obtain larger birds than the grass parakeets (such as cockatiels or rosellas), he will then wish he had made the pens wider and longer, and maybe even higher.

My grass parakeet pens vary from seven feet long to ten feet long. I think eight feet in length is very desirable. The longer the flight beyond eight feet, the greater the chance of having the young bird just out of the nest break its neck or do other damage to itself against the wire at the end of the pen. Let me state again that I know this subject is very controversial, and I am merely stating my thoughts on the subject. I would suggest that the breeder-to-be talk to as many other breeders as possible and then build a few trial pens before committing a large sum of money for a lot of pens only to discover at a later date that they should have been of a different size.

I like my pens to be of a height at least six inches higher than myself. Seven or eight feet in height would do fine in most cases. This usually allows free movement inside the pen without stooping or banging one's head. But if pens are built *too* high, many problems are encountered when trying to net or catch the birds.

ROOFING

Roofing also is a very controversial subject. I have most of my pens covered with solid waterproof roofing. My reasons for this are several. First of all, a solid waterproof roof will keep the flooring dry, and this is important. Secondly, the aviary birds cannot be readily seen from overhead by owls and hawks and other airborne predators. Lastly, the chances of contamination from the droppings of wild birds that land on the aviary are greatly reduced.

NETTING

Aviary netting is cheaper and lighter than hardware cloth and is very suitable for grass parakeets. However, it is harder to apply tightly and may cause serious holding problems if at a later date larger birds are put into the pen. Also, possums, skunks, etc., can rip it off or apart a lot easier than the other wires available. I use hardware cloth having a mesh size of one-half inch by one-half inch. I also use one-half inch by one inch, which is even stronger. The use of one inch by one inch aviary wire or anything larger is to be discouraged, as rodents can enter into the aviary easily through it. I have a friend who recently built new aviaries using one inch by one inch wire; he has had to spend hundreds of dollars (not to mention the costly and rare birds he has lost to the rats) and he *still* hasn't controlled or eliminated the rats. If you decide that you are in a rodent-proof area and therefore don't need to be concerned with this problem, I hope you will heed this warning anyhow, because rats and their cousins show up in the darndest places!!

FLOORING

I wish I could skip this topic, as nearly every other breeder you run across has a different opinion. Some prefer cement, mostly because it is varmint-proof but also for other reasons. Some do not like cement floors, because they hold and give off moisture. Some like wooden floors, whereas others wisely state that wooden floors harbor and protect rats and mice and many types of undesirable bugs. I started out using pieces of hardboard on top of bare ground, and then I built some aviaries with half-inch by half-inch wire two inches above the bare ground, using two-feet by four-feet frames with wire netting on top of the frames any place where the ground would get wet, such as under the water dishes. My thoughts on this were that dry ground should be okay if situated under a solid roof and if the birds are wormed

An automatic incubator modified for use with grass parakeet eggs. The eggs are placed in the bowls two or three days before hatching to keep newly hatched chicks from floundering about in the incubator.

Left: A typical nest box used for grass parakeets. It is 6″ wide, 8″ high and 8″ long, with a concave bottom. The perch is a ½″ dowel extending 2″ inside and 3″ outside. A half inch of wood shavings lines the bottom.

Below: Breeding boxes and feeding cups.

periodically. (More about worming in the "Medications" section). My losses have been very minimal, no more than with the other types of floors I use.

MISCELLANEOUS AVIARY NOTES

My opinion is that the open portion of the aviary should face east and a few degrees north if possible, to make use of the morning sun. The second best choice is facing east and a few degrees south; the third choice is to have the aviary facing southwest. If the open portion of the aviary faces north, a portion of the roof must be of wire to let the birds get some sun, unless an opening, such as a window, is also provided to the east, south or west.

My aviaries have a strip of corrugated plastic approximately a foot and a half deep on all four sides, or at least on the windward sides to protect the birds from the wind and drafts. The perches are usually placed a couple of inches above the bottom of the draft guards. This, of course, interferes to some extent with the viewing of the birds, but it surely guarantees the life of the birds for a longer period of time. If you feel it is desirable to put the birds on display, heavy clear plastic sheeting can be purchased and used as draft curtains. The draft curtains should hang down from the roof line.

In my experience, grass parakeets can take a lot of heat and cold, provided that they are gradually acclimated to the extremes to which they are subjected. For example, I know several breeders here in southern California who are situated on the border of a desert or even within a desert, and these areas are subjected to an extreme variability in temperature, from over 100 degrees Fahrenheit to below the freezing point. The birds can withstand that situation, but they can't stand up to sudden temperature changes. An abrupt change in temperature coupled with drafts can be an immediate killer, so make sure that you never let your birds be subjected to drafts or rapid temperature changes.

I am not saying that grass parakeets can survive an extremely hot summer or cold winter, even in those places that have a temperature range roughly approximating that prevailing in the birds' home areas. Certainly there are limitations on the degree of cold or heat the birds can stand, no matter how gradually they are acclimated. My experience is based on my handling of the birds in southern California, and I'm sure that if I lived in the northeastern section of the country or any other section in which the winter is always accompanied by protracted periods of severe cold and snow and freezing rains, I'd attempt raising the birds only in an indoor aviary or a well insulated and heated outdoor aviary. The point is this: if you live in a place where the climate is different from the one on which I've based my conclusions, be careful. Check, double-check and triple-check before subjecting your beautiful (and expensive) birds to climatic conditions that can kill them.

A grass parakeet should never be transferred from one extreme to another temperature-wise without special care being taken to insure its comfort and health. For example, if a bird is shipped from a relatively warm area to a relatively cold one at a time in the year when there is almost certain to be a big temperature differential between the two points, the bird should be housed inside until warm weather returns to its new home area and *then* be moved outside to start getting acclimated to its new home.

I make it a habit never to place a bird into strange surroundings late in the afternoon. The reason for this is that if the bird gets frightened and cannot see during the dark hours while in a strange pen, the chance that great bodily harm will occur is greatly increased. If I take a bird home after dark, I leave it in the carrying case until the morning, with a towel or similar piece of heavy cloth over it. Anytime a bird is being transported in a carrying case, a piece of cloth covering the transporting case will greatly help in keeping the bird calmer and quieter.

I always put seed, plus a piece of apple or celery, into the case when carting or shipping birds from one place to another. Some shippers use non-spillable water containers, but for me the apple or celery seems to work fine. Care should be taken to have high boards on a shipping or carrying box to ensure that all the seed will not be kicked out or fall out.

WATER CONTAINERS

I use nine-inch Pyrex pie plates for water containers, because they are fairly shallow, allowing the birds to bathe freely. This the grass parakeets love to do. The Pyrex dishes are also easy to clean. I mount mine on a piece of marine plywood, with a hole in it to hold the dish, and attach it inside the pen, but in such a way that it can be serviced from the outside of the aviary. This way I can change the water handily with the water hose, first forcing the old water out of the dish and then refilling it with fresh water. This really saves a lot of time; by careful planning beforehand, I now readily change the water in all the pens without entering any of them. I feel that this is very important in the breeding season. By installing a little trap door on each pen, next to the water dishes, I can also wash the water dishes whenever desired without entering the pen and disturbing the birds.

Some breeders claim that if green algae are allowed to accumulate in the water dishes it is good for the birds and is very desirable. They also state that the algae should be removed only after they have turned brown or red, because they then can cause a lot of harm. I do not really know whether the above is actually true; I clean mine out just as soon as the green starts to show.

If you have a glass water dish in which the algae have dried and are sticking to the bottom, you will find out that it is mighty hard to try to scrape or rub the algae out. But a piece of very fine wet or dry type sandpaper with a little water added will do the job well; so will very fine steel wool. Make

A pair of elegant grass parakeets. They are known for their swift flight and erratic and rapid wing beats.

sure that any dish on which you use sandpaper or steel wool gets very thoroughly rinsed before being used again.

There are several automatic drinkers on the market, all of them fed constantly by water pressure from the watering system. If an automatic waterer is to be used, care should be taken to select one that has a fairly large but shallow container to furnish the birds with bathing requirement facilities. Sometimes automatic watering devices corrode or become stopped up, requiring constant cleaning or adjustment. The constant drip type of automatic waterer sometimes creates a problem if the aviary is situated on very hard ground; the water can't drain into the ground and must run off someplace else. I have hard (adobe) ground in my area, so I prefer the Pyrex dish that I use. I change the water every second day in cool weather and every day in really warm weather. The open dish type is also handier, at least in my opinion, when you have to put medication or vitamins into the water.

NEST BOXES

The nest boxes I use are six inches (sometimes eight inches) wide by eight inches deep and eight inches high. I use a 1 ¾-inch or 2-inch entrance hole. I use a ½ inch by 5-inch-long dowel or perch; three inches extend outside the box and two inches extend inside. I use a concave nest box bottom. The entrance hole is centered two inches below the top of the box, and the perch is centered two inches below the center of the entrance hole, or four inches center below top of box. A quarter of an inch to half an inch of pine shavings should be in the bottom of the box. Some breeders fill the box about half full with pine shavings and other material. My experience has been that the hen will work very hard in throwing out the excess nesting material, so why make her do all this extra work when she's going to have plenty to do in laying and incubating the eggs and then feeding the young chicks for at least three and a half weeks or longer? Many nestings by grass parakeets over a period of years have proved to me that the birds prefer just a small amount of nesting material. Also, the amount and type of nesting material can cause the eggs to be buried or the newly hatched chicks to smother, especially where a lot is used or where a fine type (such as sawdust or peat moss) is used. Once again, this subject is very controversial, and the opinions of other successful breeders should be sought by the novice.

Grass Parakeets sometimes become egg-bound in cold weather, and for that reason the nest boxes should be taken down before cold weather sets in. They should be put back up when warm weather returns the following year.

One of the biggest problems in leaving the nest boxes up comes when the hen quits setting in the nest box all night. This usually happens about the time the youngest chick is seven to ten days old. In normal weather this usually causes no problem, but when the temperature drops below fifty degrees Fahrenheit, there arises the serious problem of having the young chicks becoming chilled and dying. This problem can be overcome by the use of heaters. I make my own heaters, but because the work involved is somewhat ticklish and requires both a good working knowledge of electronics and the tools (and skill) needed to put the heaters together, most novice breeders should buy ready-made heaters if they are available at pet shops and bird specialty stores.

Different books state that the nest boxes should have the opening in the box facing north. In my aviaries I do not find that it makes much difference which way the entrance hole faces. Therefore I place the boxes where I think that the birds can get the most privacy and the least disturbance, and I don't worry much about which way the opening faces.

I usually place only one nest box in each breeding pen. Some breeders place two or more boxes in each pen. I have experimented in the past and really couldn't see much difference either way. Of course, please remember that I am talking about grass parakeets only; for other species, the number of nest boxes in each pen definitely does make a difference.

I want to add one last paragraph about incubators. I have learned over a period of time that an incubator is to be used only in emergencies or tests when you're raising Grass Parakeets. If you try to get more egg and chick production from each pair and do so by removing eggs from the nest to the incubator, you'll find out that you're probably making a bad mistake. We may be able to fool Mother Nature, but we sure can't improve on her—at least, I certainly didn't. The healthiest chicks I have seen raised were by the parent or foster birds, not the human hand-feeders.

FOSTER PARENTS

Usually the best foster parents for grass parakeet babies are other grass parakeets. Some breeders have stated they used lovebirds. Others have tried using budgerigars as foster parents, but the results were very bad. One of the problems encountered with budgerigars as foster parents results from the fact that budgie chicks are nude when hatched, while grass parakeet chicks have a white down-like covering over the newly hatched skin. Finches, doves, etc., as foster parents will not be successful, because they have a straight beak, as opposed to the hooked beaks of grass parakeets, and use a different method in feeding their babies. I have known cases where red-rumps (a much larger bird) have been good foster parents for grass parakeet babies, but usually this is not so, and it should be tried as a last resort only.

Regardless which bird is selected as a foster parent, its eggs should have somewhere near the same hatch date as the eggs it is being asked to foster. The same applies to the babies put into a foster nest also, because having one or two larger chicks in the nest usually results in the smaller ones being trampled to death or not getting enough food. Any time the parent birds are doing their job well, by all means leave them alone. You just can't improve on good-feeding parent birds.

CHECKING NEST BOXES

I try to disturb the nest with young chicks as little as possible. If some of the young chicks do perish in the nest box, you will be able to smell it soon enough, so let your nose be your guide. When one or more chicks are dead in the nest you often will be able to detect this by the flow of ants coming and going to the nest box. The ants never disturb any of my nest boxes unless there is a dead bird inside. So keep a good eye on the nest box with chicks in it, but do your observing from a distance if all looks well.

The grass parakeets usually sit with chicks in the nest box day and night for approximately eight to twelve days after the last chick is hatched, coming out of the box each day for successively longer and longer periods of time. If I notice the hen is not in the nest box at times such as early morning, or just before dark, especially after the chicks are just a few days old, I will immediately take a good look inside the nest box to see whether the chicks are okay, and I take an especially good look at their crops to see whether they are full of food. If all is not well, then and only then do I remove the chicks to a selected foster parent or to be hand-fed by someone skilled in this process. I do not hand-feed birds myself; I have it done by others who are more qualified to do so.

Nest boxes should be spaced as far apart in the aviary as possible. Occasionally some birds will refuse to nest in any box. Breeders faced with this problem should furnish tree stumps with holes in them.

Our birds are dependent on seeds to grow their vari-colored coat of feathers, maintain their life and reproduce their kind. Seeds, therefore, play a most important role in the life of the seed-eating cage birds.

Feeding

I buy the best health grit I can, one hundred pounds at a time. I keep it stored in a plastic container having a 30-gallon capacity and a tight-fitting lid. I use a wooden container in the aviaries, one in each pen. I add several ingredients to the health grit purchased from the supply house. I add crushed chicken egg shell, boiled for twenty-five minutes to eliminate the chance of birds getting the disease salmonellosis, commonly found in chickens and chicken eggs. After boiling the shells, I dry them in the oven to insure against mold. I add extra crushed oyster shells, ten pounds of shells per one hundred pounds of grit. I add crushed wood charcoal, about two pounds per one hundred pounds of grit. I add ground ocean kelp, which is really loaded with vitamins and trace minerals, also about two pounds per one hundred pounds of grit. Finally I add about two pounds of a powdered product containing all the vitamins and trace minerals required. There are several different brands available. It is manufactured for birds, etc., and can usually be purchased at any pet supply store.

All these ingredients are stirred together as they are added to the health grit and then stored in the plastic container and doled out as needed. It takes only about half an hour to prepare it, and then I have about a year's supply on hand for when I need it. If this procedure sounds complicated, let me assure you that it really isn't, once you have acquired the necessary ingredients, and I feel that the birds really benefit from it.

FEEDS USED

In my two-compartment feeders, I place small sunflower seed (agate) in one compartment, and in the other compartment I place parakeet mix. This parakeet mix comes in 100-pound sacks. It contains forty percent canary, millet, oat groats (pre-husked oats) and various other seeds. Some breeders use small containers or dishes to place the seed in. This of course necessitates periodically blowing off the discarded hulls so that the birds can get to the unused seed in the bottom of the dish. For a few pairs of birds I probably wouldn't mind using this method—but for many pairs of birds, no way. I keep a constant supply of horse-block in each pen. Horse-block, in case you're not familiar with it, is manufactured by Ralston Purina and probably other manufacturers of feed and seeds. It comes in a 33-pound block, about twelve or fourteen inches square, and can be sawed into small pieces or broken apart with a chisel or hatchet. It is quite soft and saws easily. It contains salt, molasses, grains, vitamins and other ingredients, all listed on the container. It must be kept in a rain-proof area, as it will turn moldy if wet. The birds really go for it, and I have heard claims that it helps to eliminate feather-plucking of the young chicks by the parent birds. It is also claimed that the use of horse-block eliminates the need for salt blocks or capsules in the aviaries.

I feed sliced apple and oranges, but the only grass parakeets of mine that will eat them are the scarlet-chested parakeets. My Bourke's parakeets are the only ones that will eat raw, unsalted peanuts. Some other breeders have stated that all their grass parakeets eat fruit, so I suggest you try it with your birds. Remember that birds are creatures of habit, so continue with your efforts for at least two or three weeks whenever you are introducing any new food to your birds, as very rarely will they accept anything new right from the start. I usually slice a sweet apple into about twelve slices, holding the pieces to the aviary door or wire by a clothespin. This makes it easy to remove the uneaten portion before it spoils. Make sure that any green food or fruit that you feed your birds is changed daily; don't let it hang around and get a chance to spoil.

PREPARING AND FEEDING SPROUTED SEED

The method for giving the birds sprouted seed that I'm outlining here sounds complicated but really isn't. The use of calcium propionate, a preserving agent, in the sprouted seed is indeed very important, and if I were not using it in the sprouted seed I would surely use it some other way, such as in the drinking water or sprinkled in the dry seed. Besides serving the important function of helping to keep the soaked and sprouting seeds from spoiling, it also has two other—and probably more important—functions. When used properly, it will cure crop mold if a bird already has it, and it will prevent crop mold if a bird doesn't already have it.

The suggestion to use the calcium propionate was given to me by a veterinarian friend who is affiliated with the California Department of Food and Agriculture. This very dedicated professional veterinarian has been the best friend any bird breeder has ever had, being always available when emergencies arise. He certainly deserves great praise for the many times he has directed breeders in my area when their birds became sick and sometimes diseased.

To sprout seed the same way I do, it is necessary to have three buckets; two buckets should be about 2 ½ gallons in capacity, and one should be 5 gallons in capacity. The 2 ½-gallon buckets are for sprouting the seed; each should have as many 1/16 inch holes as possible drilled into the bottom.

The next step is to use 25 pounds of straight canary seed, 25 pounds of proso millet, 15 pounds of wheat and about one-third of a 50-pound bag of small sunflower seeds. Mix all of the above in a 20- or 30-gallon metal or plastic bucket and stir thoroughly. When this amount is used up, just repeat as needed. Purchase also some calcium propionate in powder form. (It usually comes in a 50-pound bag. If three breeders were to go together in purchasing it, it would be a lot better, because a 5-gallon bucket of it weighs approximately 15 pounds and will last many months. Calcium propionate is used in several turkey and chicken feeds, and many bread bakeries use it to help preserve the products they sell.)

Now we are ready to start the seed-sprouting process. I will try to describe my method step by step, and I hope I won't make it sound too complicated, as it really isn't; after a few days it will then be very simple to do.

Step #1: Pour about one and one-half gallons of water into the 5-gallon bucket. The water need not be measured out precisely; just make the bucket about one-quarter full.

Step #2: Add to the water in the bucket one teaspoon of calcium propionate. This amount also is not critical, so it can be a level or rounded teaspoonful.

Step #3: Pour the desired amount (I use a 2-pound coffee can full for approximately sixty pairs of grass parakeets) of the pre-mixed seed into the water and leave it to soak for a period of 24 hours.

Step #4: At the end of the 24 hours, pour the seed and water into one of the sprouting buckets with the holes in the bottom. This allows the water to drain off slowly. The seed should be allowed to stay in this sprouting bucket in a moist condition (wet down every 24 hours) until the sprout on the sunflower seed is approximately a quarter of an inch long. I am told by qualified people that at this point the nutritional and vitamin content of the seeds has been greatly increased.

In the wintertime it takes approximately 48 hours for the seed in the sprouting bucket to sprout to the desired length. In the fall it usually takes approximately 36 hours and in hot weather approximately 24 hours to sprout the desired length. One merely has to look at the length of the sprout and adjust the sprouting time accordingly.

Once step #4 is completed, the whole process should be started again. Twenty-four hours before feeding time is the last time I add water. The sprouted seed when I feed it is nearly dry but still soft and easy to crack and digest; this is very important when baby chicks are being fed by the parent bird or birds.

The use of pre-mixed (forty percent canary seed) parakeet mix referred to as XM, etc., can be substituted instead of purchasing the wheat, proso millet and straight canary seed as stated earlier, but the drawback of using this method is that there are oat groats included in some pre-mixed seeds, and it is possible that the oat groats could spoil when kept in a dampened state from 48 hours to 72 hours. The difference between regular oats and oat groats is primarily that oat groats have been through a process that removes the hulls. While going through this process they have been partially cooked to the point where they will not sprout, and they could become spoiled if kept damp too long.

Soft and damp unspoiled oat groats can be real helpful to the parent birds when feeding young chicks. For this reason, just before I add the water to the sprouting bucket for the last time (twenty-four hours before feeding, remember?), I add a small amount of oat groats to the sprouting bucket and then add the water for the last time. Thus, twenty-four hours later when the sprouted seed is fed, the oat groats are nice and soft but of course in no danger of being spoiled.

I usually give each pair of birds about one tablespoon of the sprouted seed. If the parent birds have young chicks, I give them a larger portion. If, when feeding, I notice the previous day's ration was not all consumed, I then cut down on the portion fed to that certain pair of birds. As already mentioned, I always feed any type of wet or moist seed or food on a flat wooden area so that any portion not consumed will dry out, hopefully eliminating the possibility of spoilage.

USING WHEAT GERM OIL

Numerous sources have told me about the benefits to be derived from using wheat germ oil; they state that it is good for the birds' feather sheen, making the birds more beautiful than ever. Much more importantly, it helps to give the birds good health, and we all know that a bird in good health can weather a cold spell or a chill, etc., a lot better than a bird in poor health.

Wheat germ oil supposedly affects the reproductive system, increasing egg production. However it works, I know that I have encountered much better breeding results after I started using wheat germ oil. One word of caution, though— I have been informed by good sources that too little wheat germ oil is far better than too much! Too much can cause liver damage and other problems.

Other breeders use it in various ways. Some make a cornbread type of concoction with wheat germ oil, vitamins and other ingredients. Others put a small amount on the dry seed they feed. This method seems as if it would make it difficult to spread it evenly on the seed, and I also am concerned about the treated seed's going rancid if not consumed readily. Other breeders spread it on slices of wheat bread, sometimes also adding other ingredients. The method I use is buying a 20-ounce package of frozen cut corn. (Cut corn is kernels pre-cut from the cob and packaged for sale.) I put this corn into a bowl, add hot water and stir. I then pour the water off and repeat the process. By this time the frozen kernels are somewhere near room temperature. I then drain off all water and add one tablespoon of wheat germ oil, stirring thoroughly for a minute or two. I then feed the corn to the birds, about twenty kernels per pair of birds. Usually I will add the corn with wheat germ oil on it to the bucket of sprouted seed just before feeding time. I stir it up really good. This method saves one trip through the aviaries, and if you have a lot of pens, each trip that can be saved is really appreciated. I feed the corn with wheat germ oil on it every fourth day.

Damp or wet feed or feed with wheat germ oil on it should *never* be put in deep containers; in a deep container it spoils too easily. For that reason, as mentioned earlier, I like feeders with a flat top. This is where I place the sprouted seed and corn. The next night the unconsumed seed is dried out and swept off before the next portion is fed.

VITAMINS

Many breeders feed their birds spray millet. Others feed meal worms. Others feed grated hard-boiled eggs. Some breeders feed small dog food kibbles. I myself use the small dog food kibbles. Kibbles have a good protein value and are loaded with vitamins and trace minerals. I feed them in a soft dampened state, mixed in with the sprouted seed. I merely place the desired amount in its dry form into the sprouting bucket and then fill the bucket with water twenty-four hours before feeding time. By the time the mixture is fed the next day, all the water has drained out, and the sprouted seed and

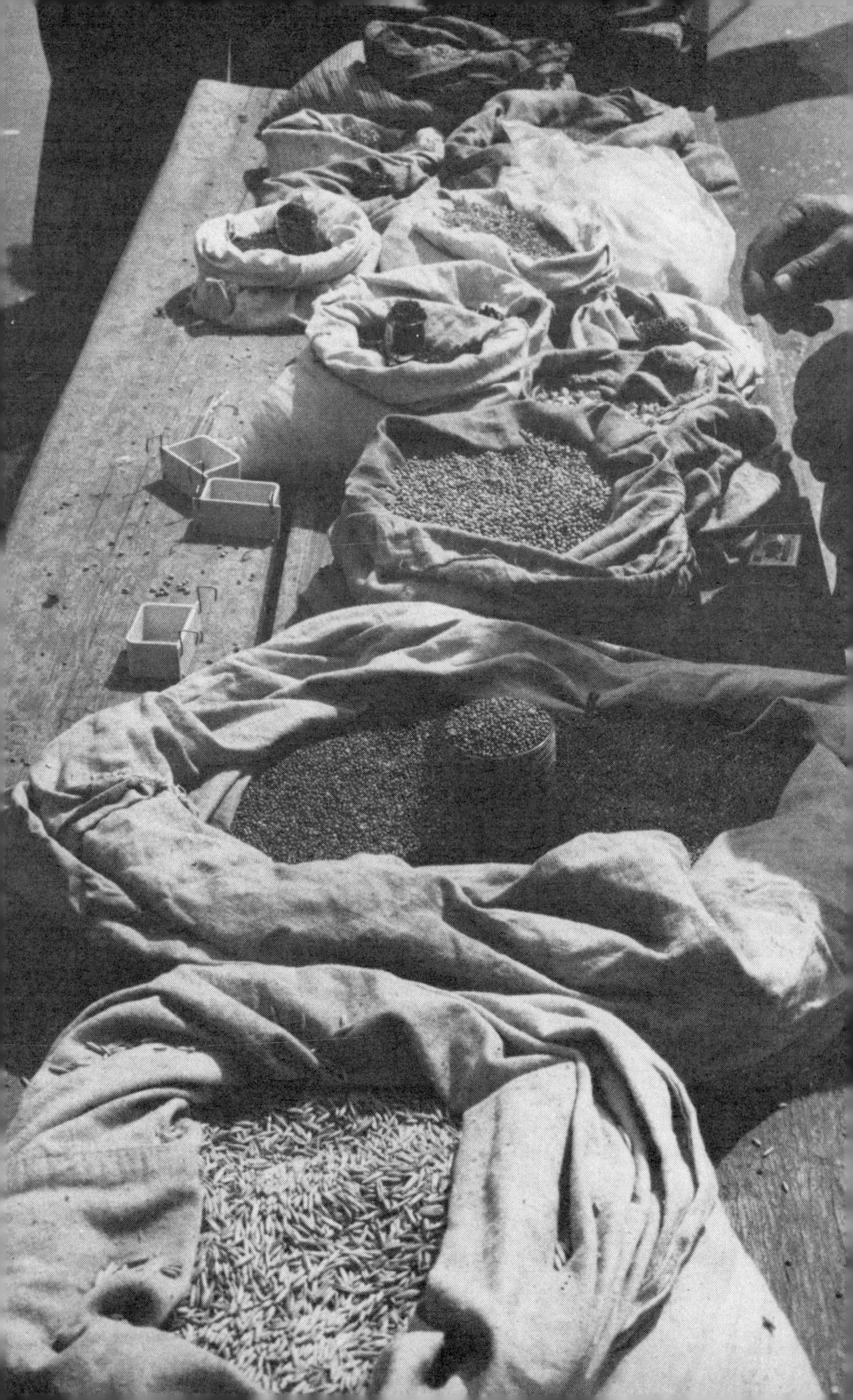

dog kibbles are still moist and soft, making it really convenient for the parent birds to partake of and ideal for feeding their young chicks. Every third or fourth day, I add about one tablespoon of the powdered product containing all the vitamins and trace minerals to the sprouted seed, stirred thoroughly, just before feeding.

Many more chapters could be written here, describing other feeding methods used by others, including dry powdered vitamins and trace minerals used, also many types of liquid vitamins that are sprayed onto the seeds or added to the drinking water. I have tried to relate to new breeders the different foods and additives that I use for my birds, and I suggest that they also confer with other breeders as to the different methods used by them.

Opposite: Seeds should be fresh and reasonably free of dust; they should not be contaminated by foreign matter of any kind. **Below:** Lack of vitamins and other food supplements gives rise to various symptoms of disease or inability to produce offspring.

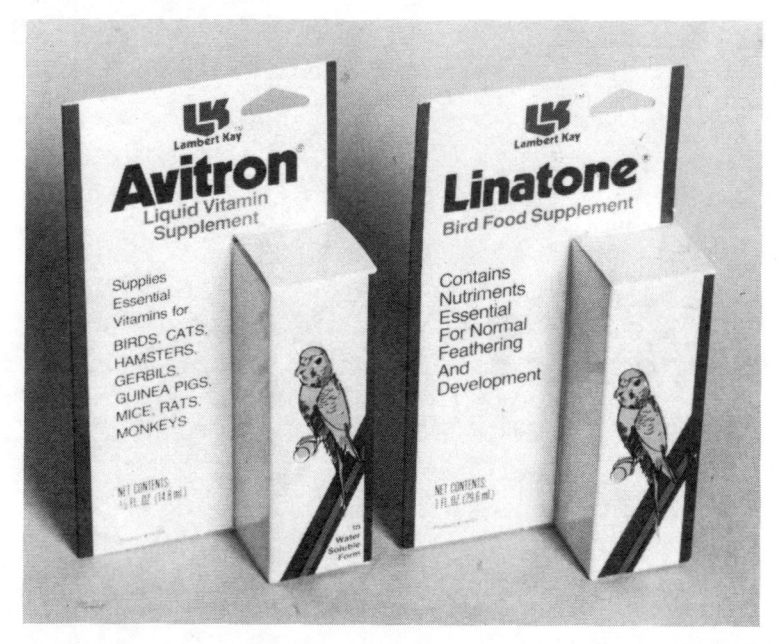

Grass parakeets usually start incubating their eggs after the third egg is laid. An incubator is essential for the serious bird fancier.

Egg and Chick Data

Contrary to the information given in some books, grass parakeets lay one egg approximately every second day, and not one egg each day. At least, they do here in southern California, and I suspect in other areas also.

They usually start incubating the eggs after the third egg is laid, and not after the first egg, as also is sometimes erroneously stated. Of course there are always some exceptions. I have had birds lay nine eggs and not start incubating (sometimes called setting tight) until the last egg was laid. At other times, some have started incubating from the first day—but normally it is after or near the time of the laying of the third egg.

The eggs take approximately nineteen days of incubation to hatch, usually a little less in a forced-air incubator.

The egg requires approximately thirty-four to thirty-six hours of constant incubation before the embryo starts to develop, so if you have a hen who sets tight for one day and then quits setting, don't get alarmed and throw the eggs away; chances are that all is still okay. Speaking of throwing away or destroying eggs if they get cold, I have read several articles stating that if the egg or embryo is allowed to cool off anytime during the first thirteen or fourteen days of incubation, all is lost. Don't you believe it! I have removed fertile cooled-off or actually cold eggs from the nest box after the hen had abandoned them for one reason or another. I have put them under other hens or in the incubator and have had them hatch from one to nineteen days later, proving that some of them were in the real early stages of incubation at the time they became cool. I don't mean to state that they will *always* hatch, but some will!

INCUBATORS

One of the best investments I ever made was when I purchased my incubator. I think it is a must, and no breeder should be caught without one, though relatively few breeders own one. I will not mention any brand names, as there are many fine incubators on the market. But I do prefer a circulating air or a forced-air type, one designed for eggs of small psittacine birds such as grass parakeets, etc. I hand-turn the egg three or five times per day. I don't like the automatic turners that turn eggs every hour, as I think twenty-four times each day is way too much.

After the hen has been setting tight (or started incubation of eggs) for at least seven days, I will check the nest box, providing the setting hen isn't real spooky. After a little while, the novice will be able to tell whether any eggs are fertile even if the hen is still in the nest. A freshly laid egg or a clear egg will have a yellowish white shell, while a fertile egg will have a dull color, like chalk used on a blackboard. Sometimes eggs that have turned rotten will look like fertile eggs, but usually they have been in the nest box a long time. When checking for fertility after the seventh day, if none of the eggs looks fertile I will wait three more days, then repeat the checking process. If they then still look clear, I will remove them and quickly candle them to make sure they are not fertile. To candle them, I use a small flashlight I carry in my pocket. I hold the egg endways, putting the turned-on flashlight against the large end of the egg. If incubation has just started, just a few red lines will show, like a spider web. If the incubation has progressed further along, the embryo can clearly be seen, heartbeat and all. If the eggs are fertile I put them back in the nest box and watch the hen from a distance to make sure she returns to the nest. If she does not return to the nest box within fifteen minutes or so, I remove the eggs and put them in either another nest box (or couple of nest boxes) or the incubator. It is very rare for a hen to refuse to go back to nest and really not much to worry about.

When eggs from one set of parent birds are put into the nest boxes of different parent birds, I make sure that the original eggs in the nest of the "adoptive" parents have been incubating about the same length of time. This is fairly easy to do by merely writing down the date that the first egg was laid (within a day or two) of each pair of birds as they start nesting. If the eggs are clear, I remove them, knowing that with her eggs gone the hen will usually start laying the next clutch of eggs that much sooner. Several times I have had a hen leave the nest box and fertile eggs for one reason or another and refuse to go back to the nest box right away. I then put her fertile eggs into the incubator and put some non-fertile eggs (that I have saved for just this reason) into the deserted nest box. I mark these eggs with a felt-tip pen, my reason for this being that if the hen returns to the nest box and lays another egg, I will be able to determine which egg it is. If the hen returns to the nest box within a day or so and resumes the incubation of the eggs, I will then return the fertile eggs from the incubator and at the same time remove the marked clear eggs from the nest box.

While I am on the subject of eggs, I will mention here that just a short time back a team at the University of California at Los Angeles published a report that stated that optimum hatching temperatures for eggs of game birds and waterfowl were different from the optimum hatching temperatures listed in previously published reports. Most of the information I was previously able to find or read pertaining to the desirable temperature needed to hatch grass parakeet eggs in my incubator gave approximately ninety-nine and three-quarter degrees Fahrenheit. After reading this article, I started conducting tests on my incubator and I found that I had the best results by far at ninety-eight degrees Fahrenheit. I will continue to make many more tests in the future before I advise everyone to use the lower temperature, but right now all tests point to its use.

When using the incubator I place the grass parakeet eggs that will hatch in a few days into a small dish lined with soft cloth. When the eggs hatch, the chicks will not then flounder all over the other eggs and the incubator.

I have had many problems with the newborn chicks after the eggs have hatched in the incubator. Several people have attempted to hand-feed the babies after hatching, and while many people claim they do this quite successfully, I have not had a single baby that survived, regardless who attempted it—and I am speaking of maybe thirty or forty tries at it! I made many attempts at placing the chicks under foster parents who also had chicks of their own of the same size in the nest. This worked out quite well, but I was still having a lot of rejections by the foster parents. My next endeavor was to try to trick the foster parents into thinking one of their own eggs had hatched. I now take the newly hatched chick from the incubator, along with the two halves of the egg the chick hatched from, and place chick and shell under the foster parent-to-be. If the shell the chick hatched out of is too damaged, I take a clear egg, carefully break it in two, blow out any liquid matter from inside the shell and use it. I'm happy to state that using this method the mortality rate of the chicks dropped way down. So maybe we *can* fool Mother Nature.

The bottom of the grass parakeet's nest is often lined with decayed wood, and on this are deposited four to six pure white rounded eggs.

Left: Pied Bourke's parakeets. *Bottom:* shade is essential for your birds' comfort and general well-being.

Colony Breeding

Colony breeding of grass parakeets is an interesting subject that needs a lot more research. Almost any bird publication that dwells on raising grass parakeets states that colony breeding of the grass parakeets has not—or will not—be successful. I am of the opinion, while not trying to be critical, that most of the later books published have merely passed along the material that was first printed in an older publication. As more birds have been raised in captivity generation after generation, I'm sure that the birds' habits have changed from those in the wild in many ways and will continue to change even more in the future. In any event, here is some information about results obtained from the colony breeding of the four available grass parakeet species.

BOURKE'S PARAKEETS: I have a very fine breeder friend in my area who in 1975 colony-bred five or six pairs of Bourke's parakeets in an L-shaped pen of fairly good size and was successful in having over twenty young birds fledged from that attempt. The next year, 1976, he increased the number of pairs in the same pen to about nine or ten pairs, and the results of that attempt were sharply reduced from the previous year.

I have another breeder friend (in the Riverside, California area) who attempted to colony-breed five pairs in a pen approximately twelve feet by twelve feet. He fledged babies in 1976. In the same pen, and with most of the same original birds, he had over 20 babies fledged in 1977. In another pen, four feet wide by sixteen feet long and about seven feet high, he placed four pairs of young Bourke's parakeets from the previous year's hatch and had 28 babies fledged in 1977. These facts can all be readily verified. So it seems to be a hit-or-miss proposition, as other breeders have not been quite so successful in their attempts at colony breeding. Obviously, if the attempt is to be made it would probably be best to acquire young unmated birds, an equal number of each sex, and put them into the pen to be used at least a couple of months before breeding time. I would strongly suggest installing at least one and one-half times as many nest boxes as there are pairs, such as eight boxes for five pairs, etc. Older birds that have already been paired off and have been used to being by themselves probably shouldn't be used in colony breeding attempts.

SCARLET-CHESTED PARAKEETS: These birds are of a very gentle nature, and I wouldn't be surprised if someone were to come along and state that he had been successfully colony breeding them. But I am not aware of anyone at this time who is doing so, at least not in any great numbers of pairs. I do know several breeders who are breeding two pairs together, some with better results than others.

ELEGANT PARAKEETS: These birds are more of a temperamental nature than Bourke's parakeet and the scarlet-chested parakeet, and I know of only two breeders who have bred two pairs together in one pen. My breeder friend in the Riverside area is going to make an attempt at colony breeding elegants, and though it of course will take many such attempts before the facts can be established, we will nevertheless get some important data from his effort.

TURQUOISINES: My experiences with turquoisine parakeets have taught me to realize that of the four species of grass parakeets discussed in detail in this book, turquoisines are the most temperamental, and I do not know of anyone colony breeding them. My friend who is going to try to colony-breed the elegants will also attempt colony breeding the turquoisines, and I will be observing this attempt with extreme interest.

I have several times placed a pair of turquoisines in a pen with a pair of different species, such as a pair of Bourke's, and another time with a pair of cockatiels, and several times with finches, etc. Although these pairings seemed to work out fine, I still maintain that the best results will always be when all the grass parakeets are housed in single pairs. Even the smaller finches can be a problem because of their continual flight from perch to perch, etc., which they never seem to tire of.

Pairs of turquoisine grass parakeets. Turquoisines have proved to be excellent aviary birds, being quite hardy and always willing to breed.

Data on Individual Species

In dwelling on miscellaneous information in regard to the four grass parakeet species referred to throughout this book, I am not going to attempt to give all the data on each species, such as description of all the different colors, the size of bird, weight of bird, size of egg, etc., because to do so I'd have to look it up and copy from someone else's description. For the person who wants this technical data, it is available along with pictures of the birds in most books already published on Australian parrots. The magnificent *Parrots of the World*, for example, shows all of the grass parakeet species in color and gives extensive information about their physical description and their life in the wild. I will try to refer to a few markings or other data that may be used in determining which bird is of which sex and species.

SCARLET-CHESTED PARAKEETS

The male of this species is truly a beautiful bird, with colors of red, sky blue, deep ocean blue and green. There is no problem in identifying the cock bird once he molts into full color. The young cocks are a little more difficult to sex from the hens until the red feathers show up on the chest. A pretty good guess can be made if there are two or more chicks: the male is the one with the most (and brightest) blue near and on the head. Some breeders try to sex these young birds by the white markings under the wings. Their theory is that if the white markings are really prominent, it is a hen. So far, so good. (This is a good high percentage guess, and nothing else.) They also assume that if the white markings are very faint, or missing completely, then it is a cock bird. This is where the error is made, because in this case the young bird may turn out to be of either sex. In one instance I banded six young birds, none of which had any white markings under the wings; four turned out to be hens.

The young or adult hens are a little difficult to tell apart from turquoisine hens, but if both birds are observed side by side, the color along the lower portion of the wings is one easy way to tell the two species apart. The scarlet-chested female has a lot of real light powder blue and less (but some) deep ocean blue on the lower edge of the wings. The turquoisine female has very little or sometimes none of the powder blue (which is sometimes called sky blue) and lots of deep blue on the lower portion of the wings. By placing two birds, one of each species, side by side, you will readily see the difference. The scarlet-chested is a very quiet little bird, even by grass parakeet standards. They all have a very soft voice, so breeders need never worry about disturbing their neighbors. The grass parakeets are about the same size as a budgerigar, but surely a lot quieter.

The scarlet-chested has the reputation of being very delicate to raise, but this is certainly not so for birds housed and fed properly. They may be more susceptible to colds or head injuries, but with proper care and housing they won't *get* colds or head injuries.

They are double-clutched and sometimes even triple-clutched, laying from four to seven eggs. In extreme cases three eggs or maybe nine or ten eggs may be laid, but usually it will be either five or six eggs. Usually the hen incubates the eggs by herself, but not always. As mentioned before, she lays one egg every other day and generally starts setting tight (incubating) the eggs about the time the third egg is laid. The incubation period is approximately nineteen days. The young chicks remain in the nest for a period of twenty-four to twenty-eight days, usually, with the hen remaining in the nest box every night after the last chick is hatched for a period of eight to ten days. After the young chicks leave the nest box, the cock bird usually takes over the feeding chores. I leave the young chicks in the pen for a period of twenty-one days after they leave the nest box; I then remove them to a holding cage. This way, I know they are capable of feeding themselves when removed.

On very rare occasions, the cock bird has attacked some of the chicks (probably cocks) when they leave the nest. In these rare cases I remove the cock bird until the chicks are fledged and put into the holding pen, and then I put the cock back with the hen. (More on this under turquoisines.)

The cock bird will usually come into full color after the second molt; sometimes he comes into color after the first molt. The molting period in my area is usually in August or September.

The hen sometimes will return to the nest box and lay another clutch of eggs after going through the molting process. Usually about one pair out of four pairs will do so.

I had one scarlet-chested cock bird that had red on the frontal area all the way down to the knee area, the red below the chest area being orange-red. It was truly a beautiful bird. It died recently, and I am having the skin preserved by a taxidermist. I do have some young birds that were hatched from this colorful bird, and they, cocks and hens both, also have some of the orange-red color on the lower abdomen, so I am sure this rare coloring is the result of heredity, not environment, and will therefore reproduce. I hope to develop an all-red frontal area strain, which I understand has already been accomplished in Europe.

TURQUOISINES

The turquoisines usually can be sexed even before leaving the nest box. The adult cock bird has a red bar of feathers on each wing and can readily be distinguished from the adult hen, as she doesn't have the red wing bar. I have heard, however, about a female turquoisine that had red wing bars. I have also seen yellow red-rump hens with the circle of red on the rump, which is usually the mark of a cock bird. So remember that exceptions do occur.

Turquoisine male chicks will usually—19 times out of 20—show a few small colored feathers on the back of the wing in the area where the top of the wing bar will be. The colors will be red or orange or yellow or reddish brown or a mixture of all four. The other five percent of the time, the colors of the wing bar-to-be will show up from one to three months after the chicks have left the nest box.

Some turquoisine cock birds will attack the young cock chicks as soon as they leave the nest box. I have noticed this happens in about one pair out of ten. If it does happen, I remove the parent cock bird to a holding cage or pen, and the parent hen usually proceeds to feed the young chicks until they are fledged. I have had hens do this even while starting a second clutch of eggs that also hatched. I am not aware of the actual time it takes for a chick to be fledged, or be on its own, after leaving the nest box, because I always leave chicks with the parent birds for twenty-one days, as previously mentioned, but my guess would be about ten days.

The turquoisine's nesting habits and the number of clutches laid are similar to the scarlet-chested parakeet's habits in those regards.

In some aviculture books it has been stated that pairs of turquoisines must be housed far enough apart that they will not be able to hear or see one another, the idea being that if they're not the cock bird may go into a rage and kill or maim the hen—or maybe that she'll kill or maim him. This has not held true in my aviaries. I have one set of pens two feet eight inches wide by seven feet long by six feet high, and I have bred four pairs of turquoisines and four pairs of scarlet-chesteds in these eight pens for several years with no problems. The turquoisines are in pens one, three, five, and seven and the scarlets in pens two, four, six, and eight. I also have several other pairs of turquoisines in other nearby aviaries without encountering any problems. I *do* make it a practice not to put two pairs of turquoisines in adjoining pens, and the same rule applies to other species of grass parakeets.

The turquoisines have been crossed with other grass parakeets, and the word received from European breeders is that the young hybrid chicks are usually mules. I personally do not see any reason for this cross and therefore will not even attempt it.

I now have a strain of turquoisines with red and orange-red markings, some on the chest and many on the lower abdomen. This coloring is hereditary, and I am now striving to get an all-red frontal area strain developed.

ELEGANTS

The elegant is probably not as temperamental as the turquoisine, at least in my opinion. However, this is also a controversial statement, and many breeders do not agree that this is so. I am sure, however, that all will agree that this species is not as docile or non-temperamental as the scarlet-chested and Bourke's parakeets.

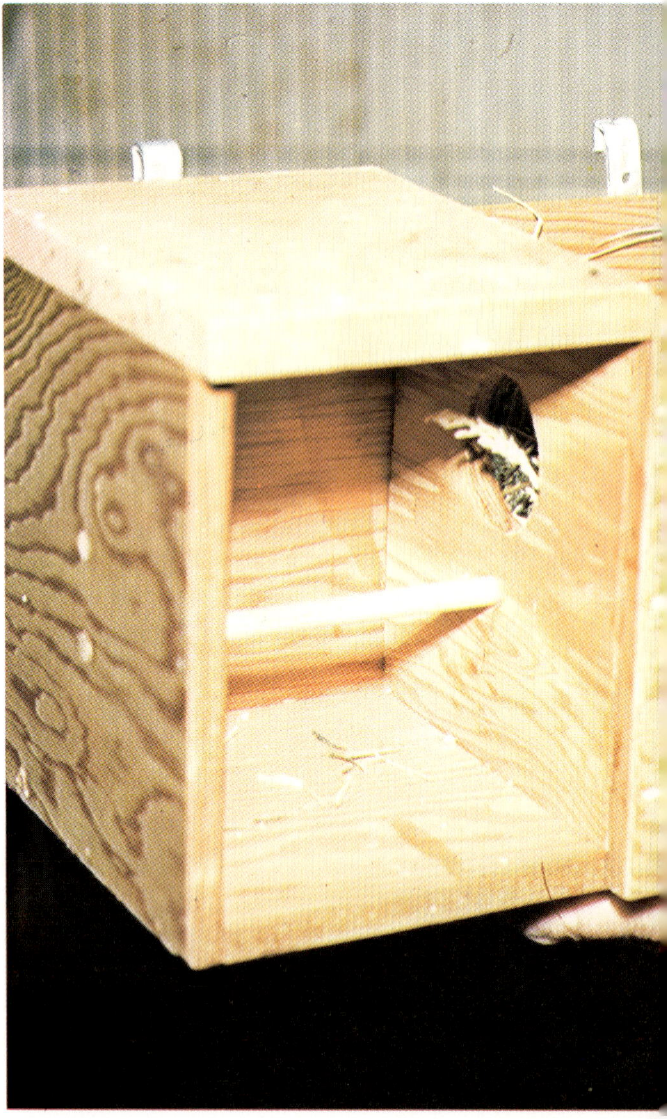

A turquoisine nest box. The hen lays four or five eggs in a nest containing damp moss or wood pulp, and incubates them by herself for 16 to 19 or 20 days. The cock feeds her on the nest.

The elegants, both cock and hen, have a blue frontal band across the forehead, just above the eyes, that distinguishes them readily from other grass parakeets. There are three ways I distinguish between a cock bird and a hen, but none is fool-proof. Many breeders have had a so-called pair in their aviaries, only to find out later that they have two cock birds or two hens.

If both birds are in good feather and health, the male is usually of a brighter or glossier feather sheen. The frontal band on a cock bird usually extends around and past the eyes for about one-eighth or one-quarter of an inch, while the hen has a brownish white or yellow ring around the eye. The cock bird has a trace of orange or reddish orange around the vent, while the female doesn't. This coloring around the vent can be seen slightly even when the cock chick is still in the nest. However, as I've already pointed out, none of these three distinguishing methods is a positive means of determining the birds' sex. Very good educated guesses, yes; positive identifications, no.

The elegant grass parakeet's nesting habits are comparable to those of the other grass parakeets: usually five eggs, usually two clutches and sometimes a third clutch after molting. Its eating habits also are similar.

BOURKE'S

One of the most docile birds to come out of Australia is Bourke's grass parakeet. It is probably also the hardiest of the grass parakeets. When new breeders or novices tell me that they want to start breeding grass parakeets for the first time, I always suggest they start with Bourke's parakeets because of their gentle temperament and their mild personality that makes it easy to house them either by themselves or with birds of other species.

I have previously mentioned the recent successes some breeders are having colony breeding these aviary gems, but by no means do I suggest this method except to experienced breeders, and then only on a small scale.

Bourke's parakeets make a pleasant whistling sound with their wings while in flight. When they are in good health and full color, the salmon or rose-pink color covering the whole frontal area is a beautiful sight to see. This color can be brought out even more by feeding shredded carrots. The rest of the bird is of a gray color, with usually some deep blue along the edges of the wings. The cock bird is readily identified by the blue across the forehead, above the eyes. This blue band shows up after the first molt, at about five or six months of age. The young chicks, however, are difficult to sex, if they can be sexed at all. The white markings under the wings are to be judged the same as in the scarlet-chested. If the white marks are really prominent, the bird is probably a hen, at least most of the time. If the white markings are really light, or absent completely, the bird may be of either sex. Some breeders go by the shape of the head in trying to sex the young birds. I have not been very successful in this latter method, so I will refrain from commenting further on it.

There are supposedly three mutations in Europe of a yellow variety of Bourke's parakeet. The first one is of a cinnamon color, and sometimes of a more yellowish color; it is a sex-linked mutation with red or amber eyes. It can be readily identified by the dark area on its lower beak, the rest of the beak being yellow or flesh-colored. The feet also are flesh-colored, but the toenails are dark. This mutation is also now in the United States, and I have some in my aviaries.

The second yellow mutation is of a prettier yellow, but it's still not a true lutino. The eyes vary from pink to ruby in color. Some of the prettiest specimens have a pinkish tint to the yellow. Some are lighter yellow than others. This recessive mutation can be identified from the sex-linked variety easily by checking the beak, which is all flesh-color yellow. This mutation is also in the United States now; I have several pairs in my aviaries.

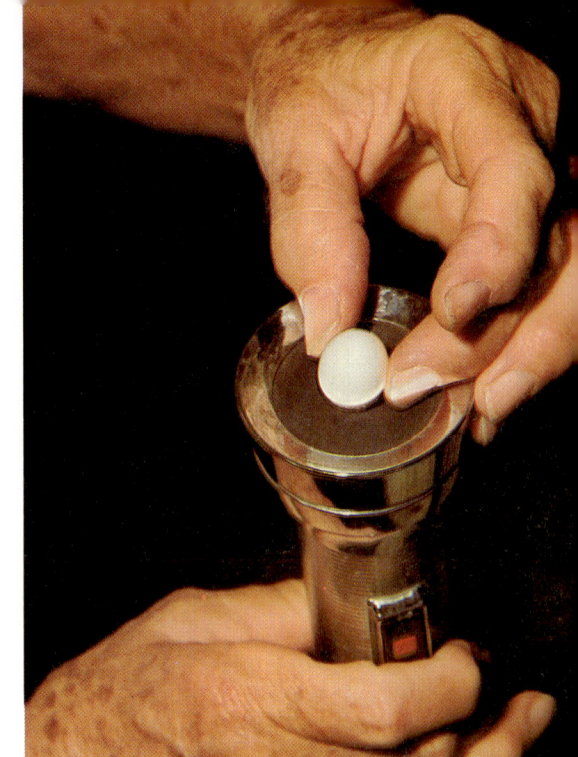

Right: Candling a grass parakeet egg.

Below: Typical grass parakeet eggs. A dime shows the relative size.

A nest box with turquoisine eggs.

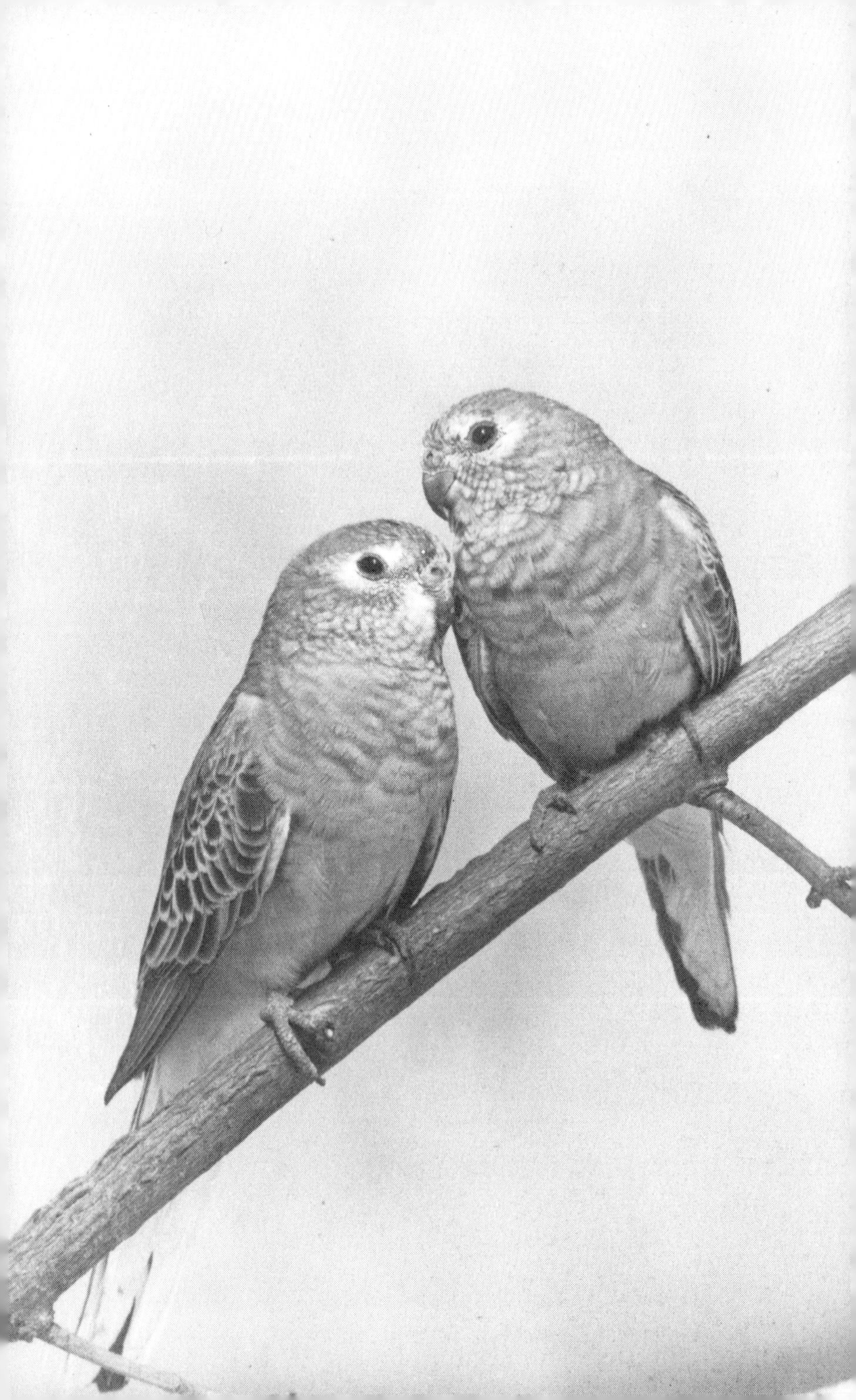

The third yellow mutation is said to be a true lutino, but I have never seen any and really have no proof that they exist.

Bourke's parakeet goes to nest even more readily than the other grass parakeets; at least this has been my experience with them. They will often breed at six or seven months old, but they should be held back for at least one year. I firmly believe from experience that any species of grass parakeet—and other parrots and parakeets, too—would be a lot better breeders if we could only stifle our impatience and breed them for the first time at two years of age or older.

Bourke's parakeets are nearly always double-clutched; they many times lay a third and even a fourth clutch if we are foolish enough to let them do so. About the only way to stop them from laying once the laying cycle has begun is to remove all nest boxes from the aviary.

This species, like the other grass parakeets, no doubt could be trained as pets to talk and whistle. I have a yellow variety in my collection that was hand-fed and never saw another bird for the first six months of his life. I named him "Poncho." He is very tame; I pay a lot of attention to him and call him and whistle for him often. He now makes this same identical whistle and sometimes makes an effort at saying "Poncho."

Bourke's parakeets (pied bird at right, normal birds on opposite page) love a basic seed mixture of plain canary seed, millet and hulled oats in a ratio of 2:2:1.

This is the very rare blue mutation of the scarlet-chested parakeet. The first one was hatched at Turquoisine Aviaries.

A beautiful scarlet-chested cock. This species is undoubtedly one of the most beautiful and the best breeder of all grass parakeets.

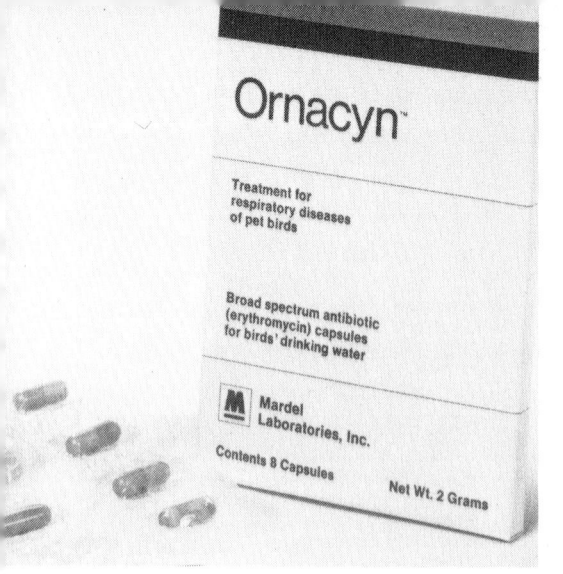

It is better to avoid sickness by learning how a bird should be kept than to try to cure him with drugs after his health has become impaired. *Below:* the proper way of holding a sick bird.

Diseases and Accidents

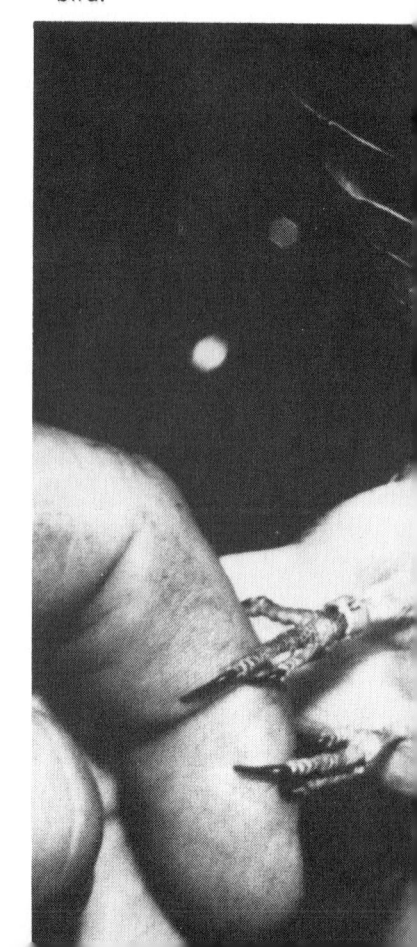

MEDICATIONS

This is really a delicate subject, and I wish there were some way of stating how strongly I am trying to stress to the beginner that I am not a veterinarian or medical doctor and that I do not recommend the use of any medication or special feeds at any time or in any way. Throughout this book, I have tried to relay information as to how I am doing or accomplishing this or that by presenting both my method and alternative methods. I'm not interested in trying to get people to do things my way—I'd just like to see them do things in a way that will be effective for them, whether they use my methods or somebody else's. This is especially true as regards medicating birds.

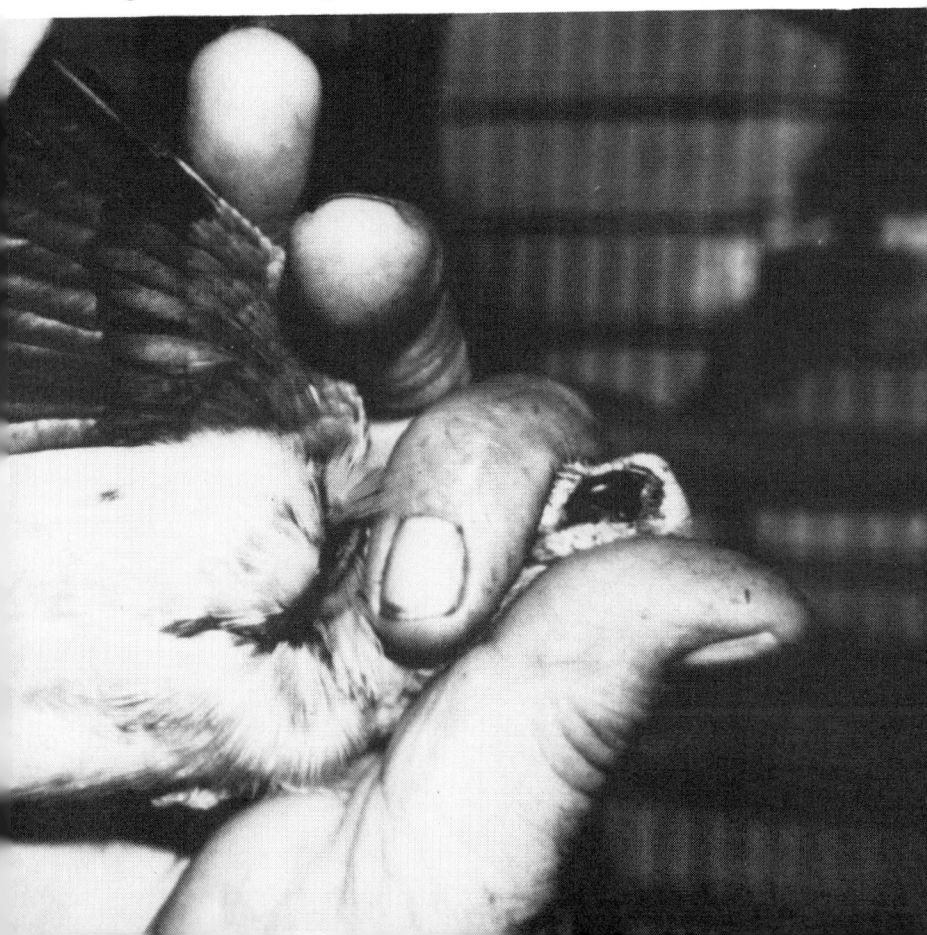

The splendid grass parakeet is a peaceful bird. Breeding results were obtained in Britain in 1872. The young cocks show odd red feathers in the crop area, but hens (below) don't.

This picture, taken in the Australian wild, shows a female feeding her young. After regurgitating his food, the male feeds the female, who in turn offers the food to her youngsters.

Nearly every medication or dosage that I use or mention hereafter has been recommended to me by a veterinarian or medical doctor and has been used successfully by me on my birds (where needed) without any harmful effects that I am aware of. There are many other medicines used by others, but I have no direct experience with them and therefore won't say anything about them.

I strongly suggest that no person, regardless of how long he may have been raising birds, ever decide to use any medications mentioned in this book or any place else without first consulting a veterinarian or other qualified practitioner.

Probably another good point to mention here is that new and sometimes better medications, etc., are constantly being produced, therefore making it a necessity at all times to keep in contact with qualified personnel.

NITROFURAZONE (NFZ): This medication comes in powder form; it is water-soluble. The dosage I use is one-quarter to three-quarters of a teaspoon per quart of drinking water. I use it for five to ten days, changing to fresh medication each day. I use it if the bird or birds have badly soiled vents or diarrhea. I am told it is sometimes used if a bird has salmonella or coliform infections.

FURAZOLIDINE (N.F. 180): Similar to Nitrofurazone, but not water-soluble.

FURACIN: One teaspoon (1) per quart of water—I use it as a medication for birds that seem quite droopy or possibly sick for unknown reasons. I use it for five days. It is water-soluble.

TETRACYCLINE: There are various types of this water-soluble drug. I use it for problems mentioned under Furacin. I use capsules furnished by a veterinarian, one capsule (250 milligrams) per quart of water for five days.

GALLIMYCIN: I use one-half teaspoon of this water-soluble drug per quart of water for five days. I use it if a bird has a respiratory problem, such as irregular breathing or a cough (yes, birds do cough) or cold.

EMTRYL: This water-soluble drug is for use in treating trichomoniasis infections and in helping to keep them from spreading to other birds in the flock. I use one-quarter teaspoon per quart of drinking water for seven days.

TRAMISOL: This water-soluble medication is available in liquid or powder form. A veterinarian has told me that all powdered Tramisol is of the same strength, whether packaged for cattle, or swine, sheep, etc. He also stated that the liquid form also is of one strength. I use two teaspoons of the liquid type per one gallon of drinking water, or I use one rounded half-teaspoon of the powdered form per gallon of drinking water, or one tablespoon per five gallons of drinking water. I use it for two days in cool weather and for one and one-half days (thirty six hours) in warm weather, unless the veterinarian says otherwise. I use it on grass parakeets, doves, finches and all the softbills and hookbills I have, and I have never had any problems with it. It is supposedly good for all types of worms the bird may have with the exception of the capillaria worm, which I am told is very rarely, if ever, found in grass parakeets. I worm all my birds once every two months, as a precautionary measure only. I have been told that birds found to have worms should be wormed twice, fifteen days apart. Again, check with a veterinarian who is familiar with the use of Tramisol.

RECOGNIZING SICK BIRDS

Once you get to know your birds fairly well you will usually be able to tell at a glance when a bird is not feeling well. Of course there are always times when a bird looks healthy

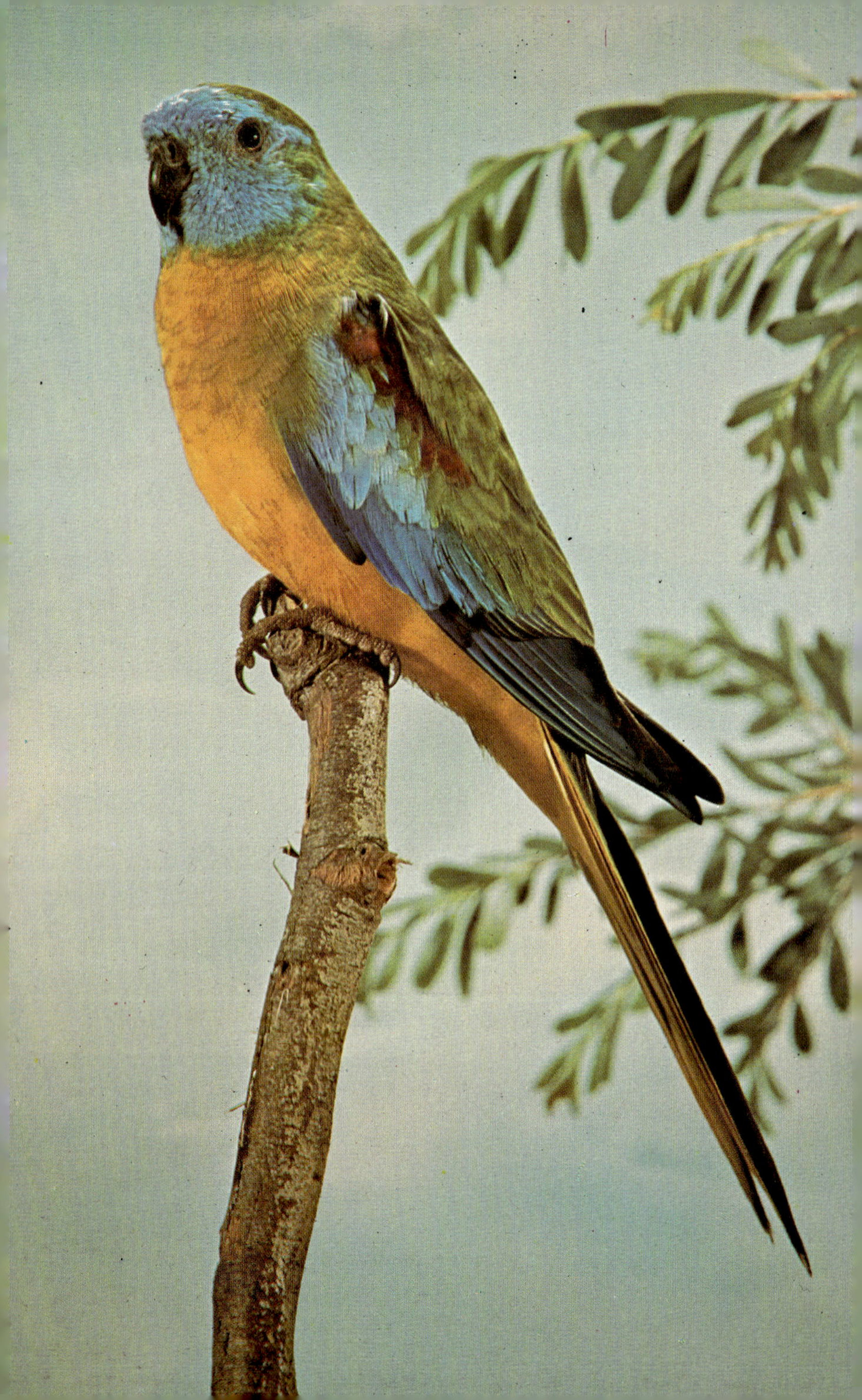

Opposite and above: The turquoisine grass parakeet is difficult to acclimate when newly imported, so it is wiser to purchase a pair bred in this country. Plenty of flying room is essential.

and fine but a few hours later can be lying on the floor dead.

If a bird is on the perch, standing on one leg, and sometimes with the feathers on the upper portion of the back and chest fluffed out, and its head resting in behind its wing, it is probably fine, just napping or resting. If both the legs are on the perch and the feathers are fluffed up all over, regardless of whether its eyes are closed or not, you usually can be sure it is sick. And if it is down on the floor of the cage, staying in one spot and not pecking at feed on the floor, there is no doubt that it is sick.

When I determine that a bird is sick, I catch it and give it a close examination, looking for signs of diarrhea or irregular breathing or signs of a cold or drainage from the beak or nose. The first thing I do then is to put the bird into a heated hospital cage and give it medicated seed or water; sometimes I give the medication directly in the beak with an eye dropper.

If the bird is a hen, I check to make sure it is not eggbound. This can be confirmed by gently feeling the pelvic area for a lump-like condition; the condition also can usually be detected by looking closely at the bird. If it is egg-bound, I warm up some mineral oil or olive oil or whatever is available and insert some oil *very carefully* into the vent, making sure not to insert the eye dropper too far into the vent, thus breaking the egg and causing the bird to die. I also put a few drops in the beak, to be swallowed by the bird. This latter method also can cause the death of the bird by going down the wrong area of the throat and into the lungs. In order to eliminate this possibility, I let a few drops run down the upper beak along the side of the mouth, and it usually will then go in the bird's mouth and be normally swallowed.

Certainly, when in doubt as to which medication should be used, by all means consult your veterinarian.

I've noticed that the body of a very sick bird is nowhere as warm as usual; this is especially true of the ones that are discovered on the floor of the aviary. Putting the sick or ailing bird into a heated area is probably the most important thing to be done—it's certainly one of the *first* things that should be done.

HOSPITAL CAGES

I use a temperature of approximately 85 degrees F. in my hospital cage. There are many types of hospital cages, some better than others. No doubt the adjustable thermostat-controlled heat type is the best. It can be purchased from different manufacturers, and many breeders build their own. The important thing, and certainly a must, is having one available.

For grass parakeets, the hospital cage I use works quite well. I use a small budgie-type cage, and under this cage I place an electric heating pad, covered with a towel or something so that it won't become soiled by droppings or spills, etc. I wrap towels around and over the top of the cage, with only a small opening in the front for air and some light. The nice thing about the heating pad is that it has three settings, high, medium and low. I set the control switch on high for about half an hour to heat the cage as fast as possible, then change the heat control switch to medium. This appears to be the right amount of heat needed without harming the bird. I leave the heat on at the medium mark for several days, until the bird appears to be quite lively and nearly back to normal. I then change the temperature control to low and leave it at this setting for one more day, and then I shut all heat off and wait again for two or more days. If by then the bird still appears to be normal, I remove it from the hospital cage and put it back into its original pen. If the bird had been hospitalized because of being egg-bound, I remove the nest box for a period of at least two weeks. Incidentally, if the bird was egg-bound, it will be easy to determine for sure by examining the cage for the discharged egg or posting the bird if it dies. (Posting means giving it an autopsy, in case you are not familiar with this term.)

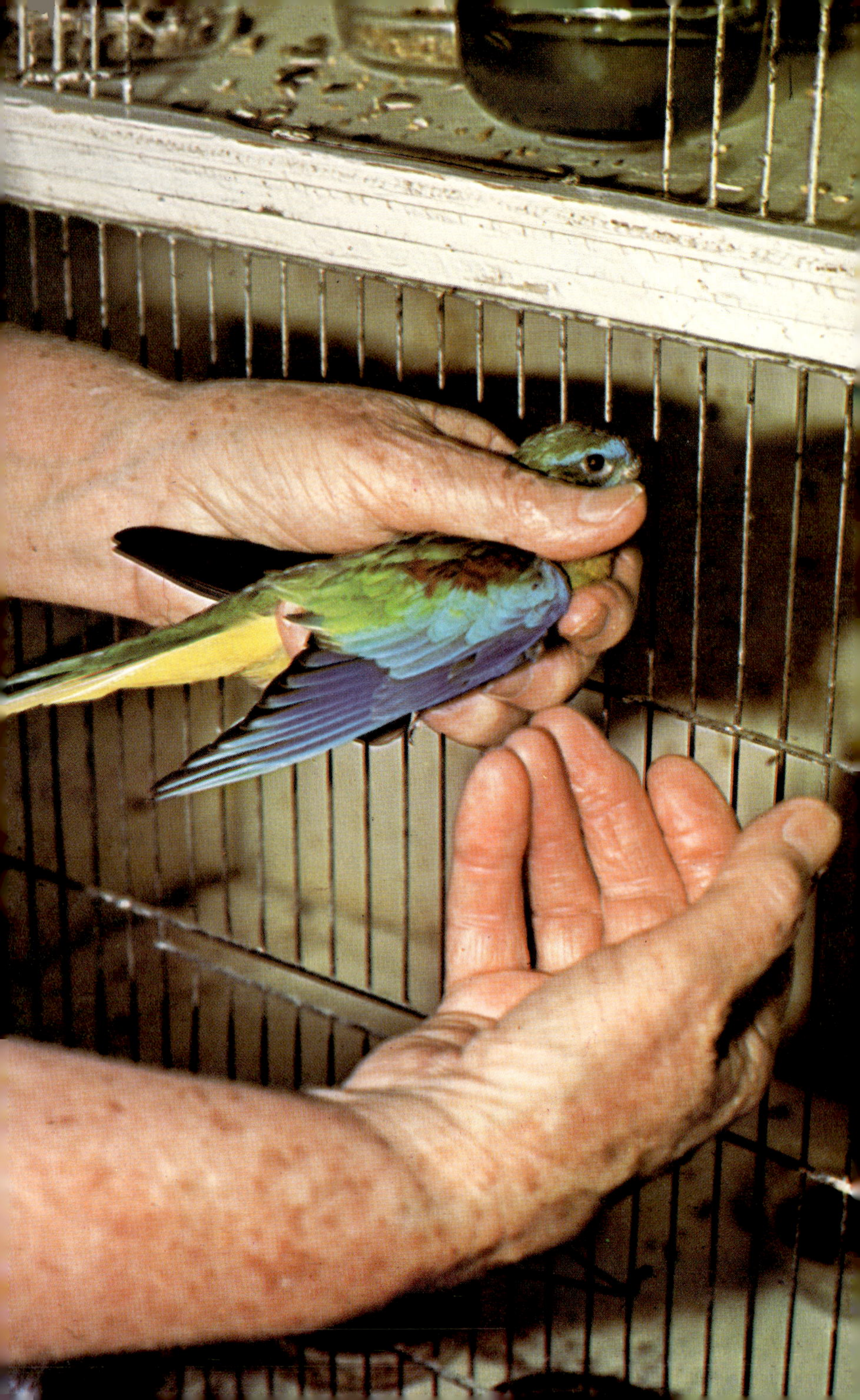

Opposite and above: Young turquoisine grass parakeet. Note the slender wings. This species has a flight that is swift with some undulation. The flight pattern consists of periods of fast wing beats interspersed with short periods of motionless glide. This way it creates an over-all fluttering impression.

Dimensions in inches.

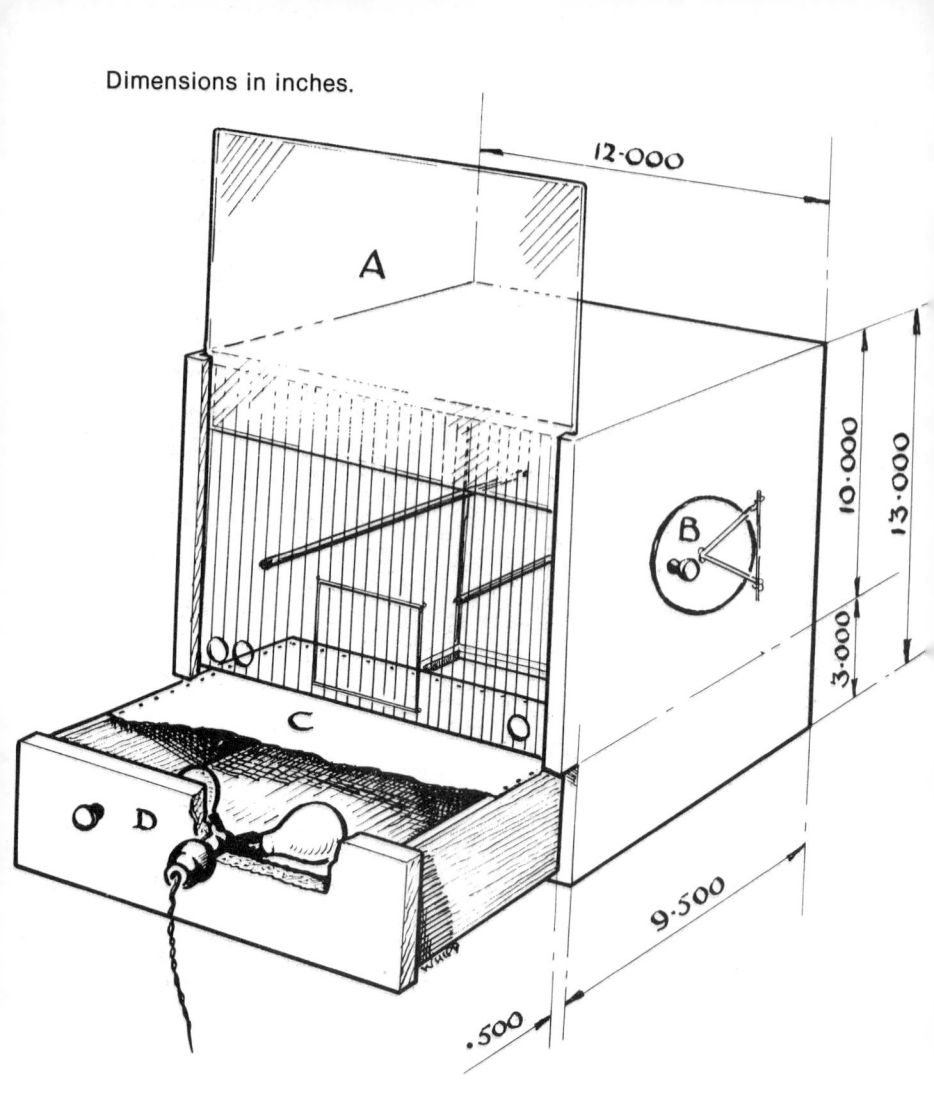

A hospital cage comes in very handy when temperature control with provision for extra heat, complete isolation, freedom from draft and disturbances, and facilities for individual handling and attention are needed.

POSTING BIRDS

In nearly every instance in which a bird dies, I have the dead bird posted. It is very reasonable in cost, usually, and it is very important. If the bird died of something that is contagious, the rest of the birds in or near the contaminated aviary can be treated and usually saved from death. By having dead birds posted, the breeder can become familiar with the different diseases that are encountered, such as psittacosis, salmonellosis, pseudomoniasis, gout, Newcastle, trichomoniasis, etc., and also learn the medications needed for different sicknesses. It was through the veterinarian whom I previously referred to as a breeder's best friend that I learned about the use of calcium propionate for protecting sprouted seed and combating crop mold; I also learned from him the benefits to be gained by using Tramisol worming powder, plus the correct use of the other mentioned medications. I have no way of determining just how many birds were spared by these different medications, but I'm sure it has been many over a period of time.

Usually, when a bird is droopy-acting, or even actually sick, it is wise to gather up some of the droppings and have them inspected by a reliable veterinarian (preferably a bird-oriented veterinarian) for possible worm eggs or bacteria, etc. The veterinarian can then probably prescribe the proper medication and dosage needed to cure the problem, or at least arrest it.

A good example of this is the disease salmonellosis. Although the birds that are infected by it cannot be cured, medication put on the seed or in the water they drink will usually insure that the eggs to be laid and the young chicks hatched thereafter will be protected from the disease.

Left: The scarlet-chested cock is truly one of the world's most beautiful birds.

Below, left: A young scarlet-chested chick already showing an unusual orange patch on the lower abdomen. **Center:** The rare blue mutation of the scarlet-chested. **Right:** A red mutation of the scarlet-chested (cock). The red coloring under the throat is normal, but the red below the belly is the result of special inbreeding.

Genetics

Briefly, the field of genetics usually is very complicated to the novice breeder, and also to many of the more experienced breeders. When the reader advances to studies that refer to genes, dominant and recessive colors, sex-linked colors, X and Y chromosomes, egg cells, homozygous, heterozygous, phenotypes and genotypes and many other strange terms, it usually winds up with the student throwing up his hands and saying to heck with it. Most of these genetic articles can be absorbed and understood only by someone willing to make the effort to do the groundwork necessary to understand them.

Nevertheless, we who strive to breed birds are going to have to have some knowledge of at least the fundamentals of heredity if we are going to accomplish good breeding results. Also, once we really get into it, the going becomes much easier and much, much more interesting.

I started out in my studies of genetics by purchasing a budgerigar handbook, because the books pertaining to budgerigars have the most written material on genetics that I could find anywhere. I also obtained a list from a knowledgeable breeder containing the theoretical color results I would obtain with different matings, such as green cock versus blue hen—all chicks will be green in color, but will be split to blue, regardless of sex. The blue would not be visible but could be passed on to future generations.

I then studied this list quite often and often went back to the genetics chapter in the budgie handbook to see whether I could find out why the breeding results would be this way. I also asked many, many questions on this subject from one of the most knowledgeable bird breeders I have ever had the pleasure to acquire friendship with, Mr. David West, of Montebello, California. Mr. West has been breeding birds for approximately forty years and is one of the world's finest and most knowledgeable breeders of psittacines.

With the results I have obtained through these three methods I used to gain a knowledge of genetics, I am now able to understand most of the basic rules pertaining to grass parakeet genetics and am able to pair off certain birds to acquire desired results.

If I were to make an effort to print my knowledge of genetics for the reader's benefit, it would probably be the worst mess of printed matter anyone had accomplished, so I will refrain from doing this. I am, however, going to pass along a few facts pertaining to heredity in birds. If you don't understand, you can start asking questions as I did, and then you too will start to acquire certain knowledge sorely needed when breeding birds.

Most bird breeders have heard of "genes," which have been defined as units of inheritance. Genes are carried within chromosomes and can be pictured as minute disks arranged like a string of beads and constituting the body of the chromosome. A chromosome, therefore, consists of innumerable tiny, flat units called genes. Most genes, as for instance color genes, act in groups.

The genes for normal colors such as green, blue, gray, etc. are carried on chromosomes that are not involved with the sex of the bird. Other colors, however, are carried on the sex chromosomes and thus are referred to as sex linked colors. Characters passed on from parents to offspring by the genes in other than the sex chromosomes will be inherited by the young males and females alike. They are "normal" birds, which means they are not sex linked. Characters passed on by the genes in the sex chromosomes will show a sex-linkage. Such birds, when bred to birds of normal colors, will, in certain matings, produce young cocks of one color and young hens of another color. Or the young cocks will look normal but be split to the sex linked variety. The young hens, if normal-looking, will not be split to a sex linked variety but may be split to another color. Most albinos, lutinos, cinnamons, yellow red rumps, etc., are sex linked colors.

The male bird has two identical X sex chromosomes. If he is visually any of the sex linked colors, he therefore must carry that sex linked color on both his X sex linked chromosomes. If he had the sex linked color on only one X sex chromosome, he then would be of a normal color such as gray, green or blue, but would be *split* to the sex linked color even though it would not be visible, and could pass it on to future generations.

The term split means a bird carries two or more colors, with only the dominant color showing, and the other one or more colors hidden, but being able to be passed on to some future chick. So a bird can only be split to a recessive (= hidden) character, never to a dominant (a character that is seen.)